POWERFUL JESUS IN THE WAR ROOM

DANIEL B LANCASTER

Lightkeeper Books
Nashville, Tennessee

LIGHTKEEPER BOOKS

LIGHTKEEPER
BOOKS

Copyright © 2018 by Daniel B Lancaster.

All rights reserved.

Powerful Jesus in the War Room/ Daniel B Lancaster. –1st ed.

ISBN 978-1-7921174-7-3

Scriptures marked (CEV) are from Contemporary English Version® Copyright © 1995 American Bible Society. All rights reserved.

Scriptures marked (ESV) are from The Holy Bible, English Standard Version® (ESV®) Copyright © 2001 by Crossway, a publishing ministry of Good News Publishers. All rights reserved.

Scriptures marked (HCSB) are from Holman Christian Standard Bible® Copyright © 1999, 2000, 2002, 2003, 2009 by Holman Bible Publishers.

Scriptures marked (NASB) are from: NEW AMERICAN STANDARD BIBLE®, Copyright © 1960,1962,1963,1968,1971,1972,1973,1975, 1977,1995 by The Lockman Foundation. Used by permission.

Scriptures marked (NIV) are from THE HOLY BIBLE, NEW INTERNATIONAL VERSION®, NIV® Copyright © 1973, 1978, 1984, 2011 by Biblica, Inc.® Used by permission. All rights reserved worldwide.

Scriptures marked (NKJV) are from the New King James Version®. Copyright © 1982 by Thomas Nelson. Used by permission. All rights reserved.

Scriptures marked (NLT) are from the Holy Bible, New Living Translation, copyright © 1996, 2004, 2015 by Tyndale House Foundation. Used by permission of Tyndale House Publishers, Inc., Carol Stream, Illinois 60188. All rights reserved.

FOR TOM

TABLE OF CONTENTS

PREFACE	vii
INTRODUCTION	1
1. WHO AM I?	5
2. WHO IS JESUS?	17
3. PRAYING WITH JESUS	27
4. FOLLOWING JESUS	47
CONCLUSION	53
THANK YOU	57
BONUS	59
POWERFUL JESUS IN THE WAR ROOM	61
INTRODUCTION	63
1. WHO AM I?	67
BOOKS BY THE AUTHOR	78
ABOUT THE AUTHOR	81

PREFACE

My prayer is this book will strengthen your walk with God. May you draw closer to Jesus every day and be filled with the Spirit. May you have a deep sense in your spirit that God loves you and will never let you go.

I have included several bonus gifts that I believe will be a blessing to you. The free Powerful Prayers Bonus Pak which includes three resources to help you pray powerful prayers:

- 100 Promises Audio Version
- 40 Faith-Building Quotes
- 40 Powerful Prayers.

All are suitable for framing. To download your free *Powerful Prayers Bonus Pak* visit:

go.lightkeeperbooks.com/powerpak

POWERFUL WORSHIP IN THE WAR ROOM
DANIEL B LANCASTER PhD

I've also included an excerpt from my book *Powerful Worship in the War Room*. God has blessed many through this book and I wanted to give you a chance to "try before you buy." You can order *Powerful Worship in the War Room* at go.lightkeeperbooks.com/e-pww

If you like *Powerful Jesus in the War Room,* please leave a review. Your feedback will help other believers find this book easier and encourage me in my calling to write practical, powerful books to encourage, equip, and empower Christians throughout the world.

Every Blessing,

Daniel B Lancaster
Nashville, Tennessee — February 2017

INTRODUCTION

Grant Lord, that I may know myself that I may know Thee.

– AUGUSTINE OF HIPPO

In this broken world, it is hard for people to accept themselves. Because people don't accept themselves, it is hard to love others too—with a deep love that transforms people, the love others need to feel. If you are like me, you want acceptance and love to permeate your life, but it is hard to come by. Just saying. A friend of mine told me "hurting people hurt people" and I've found that to be so true in my life. The problem is... all of us are hurting people.

Almost twenty years ago, my wife and I started on a journey of spiritual growth based on eight pictures of Jesus. A picture is worth a thousand words and we discovered that God had given us pictures in the Bible to help us become more like Jesus. Sounds simple and it can be. I'm going to show you how to grow in Christ.

In the process, you will discover how to accept yourself and love others like you never thought possible. If you have read my previous books, you know I don't share theories—just practical action plans that have worked in my life and the lives of many others.

I'm excited you chose this book because I know it is going to change your life. The lessons I am going to share with you have been life-changing for my family, my co-workers, many others, and me. The solutions were developed while our family started two churches in America and refined further as we trained 5,000 nationals in Southeast Asia as missionaries. I've seen people's lives changed repeatedly. I look forward to hearing from you when God does the same in your life.

So, in this book I'm going to share the eight main pictures of Jesus in the Bible. Jesus fulfilled each of these eight pictures completely and perfectly. God has made people in such a way that they are usually strong in two of the pictures but need other pictures to complete them.

This book will teach you why people experience conflict and how you can bring people into unity as a peacemaker. It will look at each of the pictures through the lens of living in the Spirit, from a neutral point of view, or living in the flesh. I will show you a path of spiritual growth that the Lord takes people through as they become more Christlike. When you understand this path, the journey becomes more automatic and less stressful. My wife and I used these eight pictures of Jesus in our parenting. Raising three boys and one girl is no small task. When we had our first son, it was easy because it was double coverage (to use a football defense analogy). We moved to man-on-man coverage with the birth of our second son. With the birth of our precious daughter, we had to go to zone defense. I remember when our fourth child, a son, came into the world. We moved to prevent defense. Just don't let them score, baby, don't let them score.

Seriously, the eight pictures of Jesus allowed us to raise passionate, spiritual leaders and bring healing to the nations. We cooperated with what God was doing, rather than trying to figure out our own plans. Each child had strengths in a different picture of Jesus. The tool I'm going to share with you allowed my wife and me to raise a family filled with faith, hope, and love. By God's grace, each of our children has continued as a passionate, spiritual leader to bring healing to the nations.

No one is perfect, but God is good; becoming more like Jesus is a gift he gives those who follow him. After reading this book, you will have the tools you will need to accept yourself, love others, resolve conflicts, and help your family, co-workers, church family, or community experience the healing power of God's love.

In the next chapter, I'm going to show you how to accept yourself. Before you turn the page, however, let me pray.

Lord Jesus,

Thank you for my friend. Thank you for bringing us together in a conversation that changed my life and will change theirs as they read this book.

In your wisdom, you have connected us and will bless as we journey through this book together.

Lord, I'm going to learn even more about you as I write, and I thank you for that. You are so good.

You love us and transform our brokenness.

Thank you.

Lord, my friend is going to learn more about you and a simple way to grow in self-acceptance and love. You know I have struggled with my self-image and how difficult it makes living life sometimes.

Set my readers free, precious Jesus, like you set me free. Fill them with faith, hope, and love for this journey.

May they feel you holding them so very, very close.

Please anoint my words, holy Jesus. This book means little if my friend doesn't fall more in love with you as they read.

In your name. Amen

1
WHO AM I?

*God loves you just the way you are, but He refuses to
leave you that way. He wants you to be just like Jesus.*
— MAX LUCADO

The biggest barrier to accepting yourself is not understanding how God has made you. When you don't understand the masterpiece, He is making in you, you may get down on yourself and wish you were like "so-and-so." Comparing yourself with others will always lead to not accepting yourself.

In this section, I'm going to show you how to identify which of the eight main personality types God has designed you to be. God made you a certain way and wants you to discover your purpose. Understanding your personality type will give you a deep self-acceptance not affected by circumstances

My parents divorced when I was fifteen and it wasn't pretty. As a result, I struggled for years with my self-image and selfacceptance. It wasn't until God showed me how he had made me and how much he accepted and loved me that I began to heal. If you find yourself at a similar place, I pray God will use the truths in this book to heal you, too.

As you work through the following exercise, pay attention to what God is speaking deep in your soul. Open your heart to the Holy Spirit. You can discover which of the eight personality types you are in fewer than three minutes and it doesn't cost a dime. What you learn, however, will begin transforming you from the inside out.

So, let's start on the journey. Let me help you find the real you. By the way, doing this exercise with friends and family will make for a very entertaining evening!

FINDING YOURSELF

Start by taking a blank sheet of paper and a pencil. That's all you will need to discover your personality type.

Draw a big circle in the middle of the sheet of paper. The circle represents the whole world and every person living on it. You can find the eight personalities throughout the world in every country and culture.

Next, draw a line from left to right and cut the circle in half. On the left side of the circle write the word "task" and on the right side of the circle write the word "people." Draw a short, vertical line to cut the line in half like the picture on the next page.

The world has two basic types of people: task-oriented and people-oriented. The horizontal line represents all those people. Task-oriented people say, "Let's get the work done and then we will play." People-oriented people say, "Let's figure out a way to make this work fun."

Put a dot on the line at the place that best represents the person you are. Before you choose, though, let me make a few comments about this line. First, after God created humanity, He said, "It is good." Wherever you placed yourself on the line—more task-oriented or relationship-oriented—is good. God has created you in a certain way for his glory.

Second, every person has "task" and "people" qualities within them. The line shows which one you stress more. If you are on the "task" side, it doesn't mean you don't care about people, and the other way around. People can care a great deal for others and be task-oriented. People-oriented people can still get the job done.

The last direction I'll give is you can't choose the middle. Sorry. I know you may be half-and-half, but please pick one side or the other. I feel your pain because I have the same trouble.

Okay. It's time to decide where you are on the circle. I have drawn a dot on the task/people line as an example of how a person slightly more task-oriented would choose.

TASK ———●——————— PEOPLE

Now, draw a line from the top of the circle to the bottom, making four parts. Label the top of the circle as "extrovert" and the bottom "introvert."

Every person in the world also falls into one of two additional groups: outward-oriented or inward-oriented. Neither group is better than the other one. This is just the way God made people.

Extroverts know many people a little and draw energy from relating with other people. Introverts know a few people well and derive their energy from being alone. If you "never met a stranger," you are an extrovert. If you "think carefully before you speak," you are an introvert.

Choose a point on the extrovert/introvert line that best represents the real you. If you are very outgoing, pick near the top of the circle. If you are private, choose near the bottom of the circle. Again, you can't select the middle. You'll see why in a second.

```
              EXTROVERT

         ┌────────┬────────┐
       ╱          │          ╲
      │           ●           │
TASK  ├─────●─────┼───────────┤  PEOPLE
      │           │           │
       ╲          │          ╱
         └────────┴────────┘

              INTROVERT
```

The next step is to discover where on the circle your two marks intersect. Look at the diagram to see what I'm describing as I give you the instructions.

Draw a dotted line from the dot you drew on the task/people parallel to the extrovert/introvert line until you are right across from your extrovert/introvert dot.

Then, draw a dotted line across from the extrovert/introvert line until you meet the first dotted line you created. Put a star where they come together. This star will help you discover which of the eight personality types you are in a few moments.

The final step before we talk about the eight personality types is to draw two diagonal lines (an "X") across the circle.

Your circle should now have eight equal pieces and look a little bit like a pizza. Here is a diagram to help you complete this step:

Congratulations! You now have a simple diagram that represents the world with eight different personality types. Now, let's look at short descriptions of each personality type. I'll give you a thumbnail sketch of each one so you can compare the diagram with your own experience. Feel free to read the description of the personality type where your star falls. Then, read the descriptions of the different personality types of people in your life.

A SOLDIER

Soldiers are high task-oriented people and a little more extrovert than introvert. They are independent and don't like to depend on others. Soldiers know how to procure results and what steps need to be taken to achieve victory. Determined and honorable, soldiers suffer willingly for what they believe in.

Never afraid to share their opinion, soldiers tell you exactly what they are thinking and don't mind pushing people past their comfort zone to achieve greater goals.

Soldiers find their motivation in protecting others and doing heroic deeds.

A SEEKER

Seekers are high extroverts and slightly more task-oriented than relationship-oriented. They have goals and are always working at achieving them. Seekers have "never met a stranger" and enjoy networking with others to achieve greater results.

Appearance is important to seekers and they like to dress for success. Seekers are friendly and make a good first impression on others. They seek new places, opportunities, and people, and thrive on variety. They work at being the best in whatever they do.

A SHEPHERD

Shepherds are high extroverts and slightly more people-oriented than task-oriented. They enjoy new experiences and often are the life of the party. Shepherds see the big picture, but are also good at noticing the emotional health of others. They see the spiritual needs of others and enjoy leading groups.

Shepherds excel at encouraging others and are determined—once a shepherd sets their mind to a task, you can count on it getting done. Shepherds sometimes catch themselves thinking about several tasks or ideas at the same time.

A SOWER

Sowers are high people-oriented people and a little more extrovert than introvert. They enjoy investing in others and helping them grow into their full potential. Sowers start conversations easily and are known as thoughtful and giving people.

Sowers express their emotions openly and make good counselors or mentors. Striving to help others grow in their faith, Sowers focus on their inner life with God. Sowers are on a lifelong program of self-improvement.

A SON OR DAUGHTER

Sons or daughters are high people-oriented people and a little more introvert than extrovert. They like to create an environment where everyone feels safe. Sons/daughters seek unity and want everyone in the group to feel like they are a part of the family.

Sons/daughters enjoy working, but are good at helping others to relax. They don't like conflict and will often give in to save the peace. Peacemakers at heart, sons/daughters are good at helping others make up their differences and work together.

A SAINT

Saints are high introverts and slightly more people than taskoriented. They are the moral voice of the community and work to end injustice. Helping people connect with God in genuine ways is important to Saints. They sometimes feel lonely even when they are surrounded by a group of people.

Saints consistently work on their inner life and can accurately detect the motives of others. Sometimes moody or impatient, Saints can struggle to work on a team. Saints find special joy in helping others find God.

A SERVANT

Servants are high introverts and slightly more task than people-oriented. They are good at seeing the physical needs of people and meeting them. Servants like to work behind the scenes and do not enjoy being in the spotlight. They want to know the expected outcome and do not like confusion.

Servants are hard workers, doing whatever it takes to get the job done. They have a big heart for hurting people and seek to meet those needs in important ways.

A STEWARD

Stewards are high task-oriented people and a little more introvert than extrovert. They like to focus on details and figure out how organizations work. Stewards see the best ways to organize resources like time, money, and people. They are wise and practical. Problem-solving is their specialty.

Stewards enjoy fine-tuning existing programs and policies until they are "just right." Their minds are intense and active and curious. Stewards know a lot about different areas and enjoy helping others with their expertise.

▼ ▼ ▼ ▼ ▼

The first step in accepting yourself is understanding how God made you. In this section, I showed you an easy way to discover which of the eight main personality types you are. This approach is simple, doesn't cost anything, and easy to teach others. In fewer than two minutes, anyone can discover their personality type.

I've shared this with over 5,000 people so far and God has used it to help people accept themselves and start accepting those different from themselves. Accepting others is the first step in loving them. My prayer is that you will do this exercise with your family and friends. Begin the joyful journey of understanding yourself and loving others.

Why has God created eight different kinds of people in the world? The answer may surprise you, but also set you on the best path to really accept yourself. Turn to the next chapter to discover how Jesus wants to help you be the person God made you to be.

2
WHO IS JESUS?

I didn't grow up in a Christian home. God saved me from my sins and myself when I was fourteen years old. Even after I was saved I knew about Jesus, but I didn't really know Him in a personal way for many years. Sadly, during forty years of ministry, I've met many people in the same place.

In this chapter, you are going to discover what Jesus is like. I want you to know Jesus in an intimate and life-giving way. I want Him to be more to you than a name in a book or someone you talk about but don't know. The good news is Jesus wants all people to know Him like that.

My wife and I spent six months studying every passage in the Old and New Testament that mentioned Jesus. We kept asking ourselves, "How can we help our children grow in their faith to become like Jesus?" This question prompted our study and led to the eight most common pictures of Jesus in the Bible. A picture is worth a thousand words and these eight pictures provide the key to becoming more Christlike.

In this chapter, you will learn what it means to have Jesus dwelling within you and how he can help you grow as a believer. You will learn how to accept your place in the body of Christ and celebrate who God has made you. You will realize that God has granted everything you need to be strong and confident because Jesus lives in you.

My prayer is that you will finish this chapter refreshed and your faith renewed. I pray you will fully understand how blessed you are to be in Christ. My hope is God will give you a deeper understanding of how spiritual growth happens—it's a lot easier than some people teach. I pray that you will take some of the ugly pictures you have placed in your heart and hang up the true pictures of what God is doing in your life.

Let's look at what it means for Jesus to live in you and how that truth can transform your self-image.

JESUS LIVES IN YOU

The Bible teaches in Genesis 1 that God created humanity in his image. The first chapter of Colossians says if you want to see the image of the invisible God, look at Jesus. Eight different types of people exist because these eight picture are pictures of Jesus.

The good news for followers of Jesus is they have Jesus inside them to help them develop fully as a person. If you suffer from a poor self-image like I have most of my life, Jesus will help you grow stronger and become more like Him. He will help you finally be able to accept yourself.

```
              EXTROVERT
           _____
         /   Seeker | Shepherd  \
        / Soldier   |    Sower   \
  TASK |------------+-------------| PEOPLE
        \ Steward   | Son/Daughter/
         \  Servant | Saint      /
           ‾‾‾‾‾‾‾‾‾‾‾
              INTROVERT
```

A SOLDIER

Jesus is a soldier. He is the Commander in Chief of God's army. He waged spiritual warfare against Satan and was victorious. He led captivity captive and humiliated the demons of hell in his victory parade. No force of evil exists in this world that is stronger than Jesus. At the name of Jesus, every knee must bow and proclaim him Lord.

You have the greatest Soldier of all time living in you. Jesus knows what it takes to be a good soldier. He understands your struggles and needs as a solider.

You can let go of your need to protect yourself and surrender yourself to the larger plan God has for you. Look to him and he will help you become a soldier that is strong, God-centered, and Spirit-led.

A SEEKER

Jesus is a seeker. He came to seek and save the lost. He did not do his own will, but looked to see where God was working. When Jesus saw where his Father was working, he joined him there. Jesus always knew the Father loved him and would show him where to go and what to do.

You have the greatest Seeker of all time living in you. Jesus knows what it takes to be a good seeker. He understands your struggles and needs as a seeker.

You can stop pretending to be who you think people want you to be. You can be real with Jesus' help. Look to him to be who you are and let Jesus help you be authentic.

A SHEPHERD

Jesus is a shepherd. The Bible says he is the Good Shepherd. He feeds His sheep and leads them on the right path (Psalm 23:3). He causes them to lie down in green pastures (Psalm 23:2) and protects them from the wolves. He lovingly takes the broken body or spirit of one of his lambs and heals them.

You have the greatest Shepherd of all time living in you. Jesus knows what it takes to be a good shepherd. He understands your struggles and needs as a shepherd, too. You don't just to survive, but can find wonder and beauty again.

You can find the joy of Jesus, the Good Shepherd, holding you safe. You can stop worrying about making plans and completing projects; you can release your concerns about how much you procrastinate. You can receive the gift of quiet waters (Psalm 23:2) with Jesus' help. Let him shepherd your soul, even as you care for others.

A SOWER

Jesus is a sower. In the parable of the sower, the Son of God went out to sow good seed. Jesus sows the good Word of God into people's hearts and it produces a harvest of thirtyfold, sixty-fold, and one hundred-fold.

Jesus has also sent the Holy Spirit who produces the fruit of the Spirit in believers. Jesus also prunes and fertilizes his children to help them bear even more fruit.

You have the greatest Sower of all time living in you. Jesus knows what it takes to be a great sower. He understands your struggles and needs as a sower. You don't have to make love happen, but can depend on Jesus to sow love in your heart.

You sow into so many people's lives, but Jesus wants to teach you how to sow into your own life—how to take care of yourself. You can stop trying to earn other people's approval, and begin to grow spiritually. Let Jesus sow a life-giving vision into your heart and remove all the negative pictures you have sown that keep you down.

A SON OR DAUGHTER

Jesus is a son. His favorite title for himself was the "Son of Man." He is the firstborn of God's family and all believers' older brother. His death on the cross and his resurrection tore down the wall that divides people and has opened a new way of love and acceptance.

At Jesus' baptism the Father said, "This is My beloved Son, in whom I am well-pleased" (Matthew 3:17 NASB). Today, the Father says the same words to every believer because of Jesus' sacrifice.

You have the best big brother of all time living in you. Because he is God, Jesus knows what it takes to be an incredible son or daughter. He understands your struggles and needs and is there for you. You can tell him how you feel and not be afraid that he will leave you.

You can feel complete and connected to your brothers and sisters. You can be fully alive and bring peace and healing to the world. Let Jesus help you enjoy being a child of God and loose you from the chains of trying to please everyone else.

A SAINT

Jesus is the Savior. He is the Holy One of God. Jesus is the way, the truth, and the life (John 14:6). No one comes to God without calling on Jesus to forgive them and reconnect them to God. When a person becomes a follower of Jesus, they are called a saint because they walk the way Jesus walked—in grace and truth. They live the way Jesus lived—in righteousness and holiness.

The Holy One of God lives in you. Jesus knows what it takes to be a holy person (saint). He understands your struggles and needs as a saint.

You feel like you are flawed at your center, but Jesus lives in you and has made you a new creation (2 Corinthians 5:17). You don't need anyone to rescue you, because Jesus has already done that. You don't have to isolate yourself from people, but can do significant work with the help of others. Let Jesus continuously transform you and trust that he will complete the work he is doing in you.

A SERVANT

Jesus is a servant. He said, "I didn't come to be served, but to serve" (Mark 10:45 NIV). The Bible says Jesus emptied himself, taking on the form of a servant, and died on the cross for the human race's sins (Philippians 2:7-8).

Wherever Jesus went he focused on doing good, and helping the discouraged and downtrodden. At the Last Supper, he commanded his followers to serve one another, even as he had served them (Luke 22:26-27).

You have the greatest Servant of all time living in you. Jesus knows what it takes to be a good servant. He understands your struggles and needs as a servant. You don't need to fear the future and try to control the present.

Jesus lives in you and will provide everything you need in the right way and at the right time. You can quiet your mind and let Jesus guide you. Let him fill you with the faith that lives confidently in the present and is also positive about the future.

A STEWARD

Jesus is a steward. The Bible teaches in Colossians 1 that Jesus holds everything together. He is managing the entire universe, from the largest planet to the smallest cell.

Jesus talked more about possessions, time, and money than any other subject during his ministry. He knew being a good steward is key to a successful life and leaving a legacy for children.

You have the greatest Steward of all time living in you. Jesus knows what it takes to be a good steward. He understands your struggles and needs as a servant and wants to help you.

You don't need to hold back from investing yourself in life any longer. Jesus will give you the clarity and wisdom you seek. You can reach out to others for help when you feel vulnerable and afraid. Let Jesus show you how to use your resources in a way that blesses others and helps you feel competent and capable.

▼▼▼▼▼

This chapter discussed why there are eight different personality types. People are made in the image of God, and to see the image of the invisible God, look at Jesus. Jesus encompassed all eight personality types (or pictures) fully and perfectly. He wants to teach each of his children how to be complete and whole—accepting themselves and living a life of abundance.

Often, believers struggle because they haven't connected who Jesus is with who they are. As a result, they try to live their lives on their own, making mistakes; they eventually find themselves acting out the negative parts of their personality type, rather than the positive ones.

Understanding how God made you and what your personality type is will allow you to cooperate with Jesus in spiritual growth. You now have a diagram that can help you grow, but also help your family, friends, and co-workers become more like Christ. You now also understand that people have different types of personalities. These differences cause conflict sometimes, a subject that will be discussed later in this book.

Our kids grew up knowing about these eight pictures and it has served them well. They can relate to different personalities and accept strengths and weaknesses in others.

In our family, I am a sower and my wife is a servant. My oldest son is a sower, my second son is a saint, my daughter is a shepherd, and my youngest son, a seeker.

Because we understood how the eight pictures interact with one another, my wife and I were able to give our children good counsel as they learned to navigate different friendships. Sometimes it was fun discussing the different pictures and how people struggle with conflict. Sometimes, it wasn't so fun.

Now you have learned the eight main personality types, which one you are, and how Jesus wants to help you live a more abundant life. In the next section of this book, I will show you some practical ways to begin to love others using what has been covered so far. Our family has used these eight pictures of Jesus for almost twenty years. Allow me to share some of the gems we have learned along the way.

3
PRAYING WITH JESUS

Have you ever felt like Jesus was far away when you prayed? Or, have you felt like you were praying the same prayers over and over with no results? Or, maybe you just didn't feel a connect with God when you prayed.

In my previous book Powerful Prayers in the War Room, I shared how you can learn how to pray in a simple, faith-filled way. In Powerful Worship in the War Room, I shared how to start a small prayer group that makes disciples and increases your faith. This book's purpose is to reveal another way I have learned to pray that makes prayer a joy and not a chore.

Amid intense spiritual warfare when we ministered as missionaries in Myanmar and Thailand, feeling connected to Jesus was critical. What I am going to share with you in this chapter kept the connection with Jesus real and powerful. I want that for you in your life. The world needs to see believers passionately connected with Jesus and loving one another.

Once my wife and I began to use the eight pictures of Jesus in our personal lives, family life, church life, and missionary life, we discovered how much they also helped our prayer life. In this chapter, I am going to share a simple meditation with you for each of the eight pictures of Jesus and a prayer based on that picture.

Meditating on who Jesus is and praying to him as one of the eight kinds of people he created, will strengthen your faith. This simple practice will give you powerful prayers in the war room and change your life.

For almost twenty years, I have asked Jesus to take each of these pictures and fill my life with his presence. I am a sower and son but applying each picture to my life has helped me work with other personalities and grow more in Christlikeness. I don't know a believer who doesn't want to be more like Jesus. The problem is people feel as if there is no spiritual growth track to run on. These eight pictures of Christ, however, are that track.

You have already discovered which picture of Jesus you are most like. You also understand why eight different types of people exist in the—each created in the image of God, with Jesus reflecting the image of the invisible God.

Now, it's time to take the truths you have learned and apply it to your prayers in the war room. If you use the meditations and prayers in this chapter as a template, I am confident your prayer life will become stronger and more powerful.

The next sections will explore a meditation and prayer for each picture of Christ. I recommend copying these down and hanging them in your war room. Work on one picture a day as you pray. You will be amazed how

God will change your life for the better. He certainly has done that in me.

```
              EXTROVERT

           Seeker │ Shepherd
        Soldier  │  Sower
TASK ─────────────┼───────────── PEOPLE
        Steward  │  Son/Daughter
           Servant │ Saint

              INTROVERT
```

A SOLDIER

Imagine a battlefield early in the morning that stretches as far as the eye can see.

Horses paw at the earth, knights clutch their swords nervously, and a cold wind makes each soldier shake in their armor.

Across the way, the fiends of hell laugh and brag about the great victory they will win against God that day. They look bigger and stronger and more evil than you have imagined.

In moments a horn will blast, and the air will be filled with screams and terror and fighting. Just then, you see the King of kings riding his white horse right toward you.

He stops his horse before you and dismounts. His armor glistens and his sword is the Word of God.

He places his hand on your shoulder and you feel the strength of his hand, his might, his glorious triumph move through your mind and heart. You look into his eyes and all your fear subsides.

"I have this," he says. And you know it is true—truer than anything you've ever heard or seen.

You hear the horn blast and rush into the battle, knowing the battle is the Lord's and you are the Lord's, too.

Dear Jesus

You are the Commander of God's army and the King of kings. You have defeated Satan on the cross by your blood. You have led the devil captive and made believers like me more than conquerors.

You know the battles I am fighting. You know how tired I am. You know how my faith isn't as strong as I want it to be.

But you say, "I have this." Nothing can separate me from your love.

Though the waves overwhelm me, and fire overtakes me, you are my God, and in you will I trust.

You, Jesus, are the greatest soldier who has ever lived. You, Commander of God's army, are the wisest and the strongest. Only you could defeat Satan and death.

Even more, you live in me! And because you live in me, I have all I need to stand victorious.

Show me how to use the sword of your Word. Teach me how to depend on the helmet of salvation. Strengthen me and give me the breastplate of righteousness—counting on your goodness instead of my own.

Lord I need you, how I need you.

Forgive me for thinking this is my battle to fight. You say the battle is yours. I surrender it to you and will obey your every command.

Here I am Lord. Send me.

You are victorious over all.

In your name. Amen

A SEEKER

Imagine you are on a great adventure. You've packed your clothes and are traveling the world. You want to see Paris, Rome, Venice, and London. An expert travel agent arranged this trip down to the smallest detail. You and your best friend are going to have the time of your life.

You meet new, interesting people at every stop. They share their life stories with you. Lots of laughter. Lots of good food. Lots of memories.

At one stop, you walk through ancient streets with ancient smells. Your companion orders a latte at the corner café and you spend hours chatting about everything and nothing. So many people. So many places. You take your time and enjoy them all.

That night, you are praying and have a vision of Jesus speaking to you.

He says:

My child, I have made a beautiful world. Enter the joy of your Master. Explore to your heart's content but understand you are seeing only a glimpse of what heaven will be like.

I am working in this world all the time. Join me and you will discover what a full life can be like. I love you and will gladly show you all you need to live in me.

You wake from the vision with God's praise on your lips. Grabbing your backpack, you are off again . . . looking for where God is doing amazing things, so you can join him.

> *Dear Lord Jesus,*
>
> *You are the maker of heaven and earth. You have set the planets and stars in their place. The mountains and rivers testify to your greatness. The woodlands and streams display your beauty.*
>
> *There is no God but you. Early in the morning I will seek you. You are faithful and true. You have promised that I will find you when I seek you with all my heart.*
>
> *Forgive me, Lord God, when I seek after sin and find only shame.*
>
> *Forgive me when I seek my own glory and focus on my personal comfort.*
>
> *I want to have your heart that seeks and saves the lost. Too often, I walk by people who need to hear about you and say nothing.*
>
> *Show me how to walk in grace, not in guilt. Open my eyes, so I can see the great and mighty acts you are doing. I want to know you more. Give me a heart that yearns for you like the doe yearns for flowing streams (Psalm 42:1).*
>
> *I pray for those who have never heard the gospel. Lord, may you give them the grace to seek you and find you.*

Give believers throughout the world the courage and strength they need to make it through today.

You are the greatest seeker of all time and you live in me. I submit to your leadership in my life and will follow you wherever you lead.

I seek to do your will and know the power of your resurrection. I want to know you more, Jesus. I lay everything all down again and surrender to your love.

Lord, you are my partner, so help me make my plans big.

In your name. Amen.

A SHEPHERD

Imagine you have been walking in a beautiful valley with a quiet stream nearby. The trees are old and cast peaceful shade. The sunlight dances between the trees and you almost feel like you can see angels playing hide-and-seek.

Just as you walk over a small hill, you see a flock of sheep gently grazing and enjoying safety and security, confident under the care of their shepherd. You sit down to enjoy the beautiful view and bask in God's love.

Jesus walks toward you carrying his shepherd's staff. His robe is soft and your feel comfort and protection as he sits down beside you. The Good Shepherd has all the time you need and begins to share how much he loves you.

"You have given so much to others—receive my love," he says, taking your hands in his callused shepherd hands. Tears fill your eyes because you know that he is the only one who can really take care of you.

God Almighty is a shepherd and has bent down from heaven to feed you with his hand. He puts salve on your wounded heart. He carries you over the rough places. He sings over you as you sleep and restores your soul.

> *Dear Jesus,*
>
> *Lover of my soul. Precious Jesus who sought me when I strayed.*
>
> *Defender of the weak and discouraged. Great Shepherd of my soul, I need you today. Hear my cry.*
>
> *My life is so rushed, and you call me to a peaceful place. Forgive me for not following you. My life is so stressful, and you call me to rest in you.*
>
> *Forgive me for not following you.*
>
> *I have taken care of others, but not opened my heart for you to take care of me. You are the greatest Shepherd. Teach me to depend on your guidance and not my own thoughts. Help me to trust in you and not overthink my life.*
>
> *You protect me from the attacks of the evil one, because you are good. You give me everything I need in this life, because you are my provider.*
>
> *Oh, great Shepherd of my soul, quiet my thoughts. Quiet my selfish ambition. Quiet my attempts to please others. I'm tired of my frantic life; I'm coming home, Jesus, home to my Shepherd's arms.*
>
> *You are all I need.*
>
> *In your name. Amen*

A SOWER

Imagine walking into a beautiful garden. As far as you can see, trees and flowers and landscaping join in a symphony of color and design. You walk along a pathway that takes you by each part of the garden effortlessly.

Fountains and waterfalls dot the landscape and leave you in awe and wonder. Your heart is full of joy and peace. Surely, the garden of Eden looked like the garden you now enjoy.

As you round a bend, you see Jesus pruning an old grapevine twisting across a weathered wooden fence. He is carefully trimming branches from the vine. Each cut makes the vine more beautiful and fruitful.

You walk up and stand beside him and watch a master at work. He turns to you and smiles. You can almost feel the joy he has for his work. Carefully, gently, he trims the grapevine until it fits perfectly into the landscape.

"Have you been to this garden before today?" he asks. You shake your head "no" and he smiles.

"Yes, you have," he explains. "This garden is your life. This is what I am creating in your spirit and soul. When you enter heaven, this garden will be complete."

Suddenly, you see the fruit of the Spirit on the trees and beauty that has risen from ashes (Isaiah 61:3). Quietly, reverently, you sit down and find rest for your soul.

> *Lord Jesus,*
>
> *You are the sower who sows the good seed of the Word of God in lives. You are faithful to finish the work you have begun in your people. You are the Creator who makes everything beautiful in your time.*

I praise you today for the beauty in this world and for your goodness in my life. I thank you for sowing all the fruit of the Spirit into my soul.

Forgive me, great Sower, for the bad seed I have planted in my life. I am reaping what I have sown; it is more than I can bear. Weed out evil in my life, Jesus.

Clear the underbrush and fruitless efforts that have collected in my life. They keep me from seeing the wonderful creation you are making in me. I need to see that creation today. Forgive me for depending on my strength to produce spiritual results.

Precious Lord, give me a heart that leans on you and your Spirit, instead of my flesh and human desires. I want the fruit of your Spirit to overflow in me and bless my family and friends.

Show me where to plant the seeds of the gospel and cultivate a heart of faithfulness.

I surrender to your will, Lord. I'm not going to depend on the world's wisdom any longer, but fully trust in what you have commanded. Prune away everything in me that keeps your life-giving love from flowing out of me.

Make me, great Sower, like a tree planted by rivers of living water.

You are the source of life. In your name. Amen.

A SON / DAUGHTER

Imagine you are in a large log cabin and can look out and see a breathtaking view of majestic mountains. Birds are singing, pine trees sway gently in the breeze, and you find yourself sitting on the front porch in an over-sized rocking chair.

Inside, all the people you love most in this world have gathered. They are talking and laughing and preparing a scrumptious meal none of you will ever forget. The smells of desserts and smoked meats fill the air. Someone just pulled out homemade yeast rolls and they smell like a piece of heaven.

You leave the rocking chair and enter the cabin. Someone set a table for the feast with candles—nothing fancy, but "just right" for a group of people who treasures one another.

At that moment, you see Jesus at the front of the table. He is wearing a flannel shirt and blue jeans and looks so comfortable. He winks at you as if saying "I'd let you beat me in a game of checkers if we could only spend some time together."

You walk over to where he is standing, and he gives you a hug. All your life you have been looking for this—a place that feels like home and is safe. Now, you know you have found it. You sit on Jesus' right side and enjoy this special banquet he has prepared just for you.

> *Holy Son of God,*
>
> *You are the resurrection and life—the firstborn from the dead.*
>
> *Because of your sacrifice, I have been adopted into God's family.*
>
> *Once I was lost; now I am found. Once I was an orphan; now I am destined for an eternal home. I praise you today for your goodness and mercy toward me.*

Forgive me, Lord, for the times I am selfish and don't give your love to others—for the times I bring conflict instead of peace to my family and friends. Forgive me for acting like I'm not a part of your family and trying to do it my own way.

Please give me your heart for my brothers and sisters. Let me see them the way you do. Let me be a peacemaker bringing stability for everyone around me.

In this chaotic world, make my life a safe harbor and refuge for my friends.

Lord, make me an instrument of your peace. Help me accept my life the way it is and be content.

Show me how to bring unity wherever I am.

I'm forgiven because you were forsaken. I'm accepted, You were condemned. I'm alive and well. Your spirit is within me. Because you died and rose again.

As for me and my house, today we will serve you.

In your name. Amen.

A SAINT

Imagine entering one of the great cathedrals in Europe. Candles burn in the background and high ceilings draw your eyes heavenward. A small choir sings praise songs and echoes of worship weave together to form a beautiful, musical tapestry.

It is evening and the sunset bursts through the stained-glass windows and you sense the Holy Spirit in power. You feel so close to God and don't want to leave.

One of the monks sits beside you; the hood of his cassock covers his head. He bows his head and draws his hands together in prayer. Light from the stained-glass windows focuses all its brilliance on this monk. You can't help but be transfixed by his presence.

He begins his prayers softly with "Our Father." You notice that sometimes he prays, but other times he sings. Tears flow freely as the monk prays. Joy flows from his lips, too.

As you listen, you notice he says your name. You're surprised but think that it is just a coincidence. As you listen closer, though, you notice he is praying for you and your family.

He is praying about secrets in the past only you know. About circumstances you face now. Overwhelmed, you also realize he is praying about your future—events you don't even know about yet.

Jesus moves the hood from his head and looks through your eyes into your heart.

"I'm so glad you have come to be with me," he says. "Let's talk about your joys and sorrows."

Filled with the love and presence of God, you begin to share your heart's deepest dreams and yearnings...

> *Precious Lord Jesus,*
>
> *You, Lord, are the Holy One of God. You are righteousness in all your ways. You have all wisdom and knowledge.*
>
> *Nothing is too hard for you. Your thoughts are so far above mine.*

Your ways so beyond mine. In a world full of sin and darkness, you shine as the sun and source of my salvation.

Lord, forgive my many sins. Forgive my stubborn heart and feet that run too easily to sin. I can be self-righteous and believe myself to be better than others. I spend too much time trying to be perfect, rather than letting you do your perfecting work in me.

Please give me a heart that loves you and worships you. Lord, I ask for a mind that loves your Word and longs to share it with others.

Lord, give me a soul that loves you and enjoys our times in prayer.

And Lord, don't let this all be about me; give me the strength to share your love with others.

Not by strength or by power, but by your Spirit. I choose to walk that way, Lord. Your grace is amazing, and I choose to not depend on my own goodness, but in Christ alone.

By your grace, I pray for my family, country, and the world until all the kingdoms of this world become the kingdoms of our Lord and his Christ.

Only you can transform me. By your grace, I know I will be changed today.

In your name. Amen.

A SERVANT

Imagine you are serving lunch in a rescue mission. A line of old, haggard men has formed waiting for the only hot meal they will eat today. They shuffle along, looking at the floor, burdened by hardships you can't imagine.

As each man picks up his tray and passes you, the smell of nights spent sleeping on park benches overwhelms you. You feel guilty about your attitude toward these strangers. You came to serve them but find yourself judging them instead.

You ask God to help you see these men the way he sees them. You ask the Holy Spirit to fill you with faith, hope, and love. Suddenly, your heart begins to change and your find yourself smiling as you give them food.

As you continue to serve, you sense the Holy Spirit say, "When you have done it to the least of these, you have done it to me" (Matthew 25:40). Jesus is here among these lonely, homeless men.

Jesus left heaven, discarding his power and glory, to become like a servant, dying on the cross for the human race's sins. He walked among the lepers and healed them. He stood up for the underdog. He called people out for their hypocrisy. He commanded people to serve one another.

You understand the greatest Servant of all-time lives in you and loves to serve those who cannot serve themselves. Jesus' humility and heart become your strength and security. You volunteered at the rescue mission for a week. Now you want to be a servant leader every day.

> *Lord Jesus,*
>
> *You surrendered your majesty and came to this world as a servant. All your glory, majesty, and honor you laid aside.*
>
> *You came to serve and not be served. You, Creator God walked among your creation, but your people did not*

know you. Then you gave your life on the cross, so I could return to you.

Forgive me, precious Lord, when I am self-serving and don't allow you to serve others through me. Forgive me, humble Jesus, when I am too proud to stop and help others.

I want to have a servant's heart like you. You live in me; please help me release my heart to you and serve others.

I pray for people in crisis who have lost everything they own. Send your servants to help them and may they answer your call.

I pray for children who are starving; send your servants to feed them and may they answer your call.

I pray for men and women who are facing divorce, or the loss of a loved one, or financial ruin. Send your servants to show them your love and may they answer your call.

Help me not become so caught up in the details that I forget the people. Lord, I give up my plans and choose your will instead.

Let me be your hands wherever I go today. Fill me with your Spirit so I may serve those around me.

You are the servant King and I am your servant today and always.

In your name. Amen.

A STEWARD

Imagine you are studying in a library and enjoying your favorite nonfiction book. Your mind is full of new ideas and you can't wait to use them. In all your life, you have never had a day like this— a day your mind is open to so many possibilities.

As you are sipping a cappuccino in the overstuffed leather chair, Jesus sits in the chair beside you.

"Child," he says, "You are learning so much today. Let me show you even more."

In a vision, you find yourself looking over the entire universe—every galaxy, solar system, and star. Each one is set in place with perfect timing.

Then, you zoom into the solar system and see the sun and the planets. Drawing closer, you see the earth, perfectly balanced, every aspect carefully tuned by the Creator God. Every law of nature working flawlessly. Every ratio just right.

As your journey continues, you see yourself in the library and Jesus is orchestrating everything in your life in ways you never imagined. You travel into your body and see every organ and bone carefully crafted. At the cellular level, you see a whole new universe, yet understand that even here—in the smallest place—Jesus is an incredible Steward and is keeping everything together.

Jesus says, "I am the greatest Steward. I hold everything in the universe together. You can trust me with your time, your treasure, and your talents. Surrender to me and your life will flow the way it is meant to flow."

Your worries and concerns begin to melt away as you continue to pray...

Dear Lord Jesus,

You exercise authority and power over everything. You are the King of kings and Lord of lords. You created the universe and hold everything together. Nothing happens in the universe, but you know it and understand why it happened. You made time. You made all the treasure.

You gave me my talents. Everything comes from you and is for you.

I confess that I try to control my world too often. Forgive me for trying to manage what is yours alone to manage.

I want to be a good Steward, but often find myself making decisions based on fear and not faith. You give the increase. Help me to trust in you.

Lord, help me to give my time to you, so you can bless it and cause it to multiply. Lord, use my treasure to see your kingdom come and your will be done.

Lord, you are calling me out and have given me talents to invest in others. Too often I play it safe and hide them under a bushel. You are the greatest Steward of all time.

You see the beginning and the end. You always have a plan. Your ways are perfect and right.

Lord, I submit to your authority in my life. I choose to trust you and not lean on my own understanding.

I will acknowledge you in all my ways, knowing you will make my path straight. I put my hand in your nail-scarred hand and trust you. In your name. Amen.

▼ ▼ ▼ ▼ ▼

For years, I wanted to draw closer to Jesus, but didn't know how. I prayed harder, but I didn't feel closer. I read my Bible more, but I still felt distant.

Only after discovering the eight pictures of Jesus and meditating on who Jesus is did I begin to grow closer and know him more intimately. We only touched the hem of his garment in this chapter, but my prayer is you have found a simple way to grow closer to Jesus in the War Room.

If you are like me, you tend to pray in certain ways and become stuck. This chapter showed you a way to take a step toward being unstuck and open your mind and heart to all Jesus is. Meditating on the eight pictures of Jesus will open your spirit to all Jesus is doing in the world, not just through the lens of your personality.

I wish you could have seen the faces of your brothers and sisters in Southeast Asia as they understood that God had made them in a unique way. Many of them tried to copy their pastor or another spiritual leader. They felt frustrated, and believed they were second-rate believers.

Time after time, we saw believers grow in their faith and become victorious in their War Rooms because they understood who Jesus was in them and how they could be victorious in him. I remember one man who glowed when he realized that God had made him a "sower." He began to spread the seed of the gospel everywhere, and God brought a rich harvest.

So, how about you? Do you feel far away from Jesus? Are you struggling in your faith? You don't have to be defeated. Meditating on and praying through each of these eight pictures will make the powerful presence of Jesus more real in your life.

Dear Lord Jesus,

Bless my friends. Give them a vision of you and how you want to help them overcome this world. Set them free from the problems in their life that trap them and keep them from you.

Show them that you are all eight of these pictures in perfection. You live in them and want to help them become more like you. Day by day, as they meditate and pray, change them, heal them, and make them stronger in you.

Your Word is true. Your Word does not fail. Show them all the places in your Word that give more insight into these pictures. Give them the faith to cling to your Word. Transform them in their inner being.

Show them, Lord, that walking with you is not as hard as some people make it out to be. In your name. Amen

4

FOLLOWING JESUS

Here are answers to the most frequent questions I am asked when teaching the eight pictures of Jesus to others:

ARE THERE MORE THAN EIGHT PICTURES OF JESUS IN THE BIBLE?

In our study through the Bible, we found many pictures of Jesus. Just a few examples include "the door," "the sheep gate," and "the lamb." Through our study we discovered the eight pictures included in this book were the ones that occurred most often. These eight pictures occurred in both the Old and New Testaments, also. Other pictures gave further details or understanding of the eight pictures of Jesus.

HOW DID YOU DISCOVER THE EIGHT PICTURES OF JESUS?

When our oldest son was five years old, my wife and I began to ask ourselves what we wanted him to be like when he graduated from high school. Our answer was simple: "We want him to be like Jesus." But, what does that really mean? What does it look like? How can parents be intentional in raising children to be like Jesus?

We decided to do a thorough study of God's Word and see what being like Jesus looked like. We carefully researched every verse in the Old and New Testaments that described Jesus—who he was or how he did something. Something we noticed right away was that the Bible uses pictures to describe who Jesus is and what he does.

Over time, we narrowed the eight pictures of Jesus you have learned about in this book. These pictures ranked as the most important ones in the Bible for our spiritual growth.

HOW DID THE EIGHT PICTURES OF JESUS HELP YOU IN YOUR MISSION WORK?

We worked among Buddhists in Southeast Asia; their most important number is "8." We didn't realize this until we were on the field. The Buddha encouraged his followers to learn about other religions, so we encouraged Buddhists to come to a training we offered on the eight pictures of Jesus. The fact there were eight pictures made the study popular.

The eight pictures also helped us decide when we were stressing one facet of Jesus and neglecting another. Good mission or ministry balances each of the eight pictures of Jesus.

Highlighting one picture and neglecting another always leads to unhealthy activities. We looked at the full of picture of Christ as we did our work and the results were long-term, instead of short-term.

I could share so many other ways the eight pictures helped us, but I'll close by talking about how we developed our mission budget each year. We would spend much time in prayer asking Jesus to show us how each of the eight pictures was doing in our ministry. We would also talk to key national leaders and ask their opinion. Then, we would develop a budget that helped the strong pictures continue to flourish, but also help the weak pictures develop in significant ways. We developed Christ-centered budgets, as a result.

WHERE CAN I FIND MORE INFORMATION ABOUT THE EIGHT PICTURES OF JESUS?

I've been teaching others about the eight pictures of Jesus for a long time. My wife pleaded with me for many years to publish this book to help others. I kept putting off the project because we were still learning so much about becoming more like Jesus.

Holli passed away in 2016 from ovarian cancer. In her honor, I have released this book to give you a "taste" and will share a more detailed book in 2019. Please pray God will anoint the project and bless many.

ARE THE EIGHT PICTURES OF JESUS AND SPIRITUAL GIFTS THE SAME?

Many believers today are familiar with spiritual gifts, so this is the most common question we receive about the eight pictures of Jesus. The short answer is "no" they are not the same but let me explain a little further.

A helpful analogy to understand the difference is eight buckets. Each picture of Jesus is like a bucket. A bucket holds water. In the same way, each picture of Jesus holds spiritual gifts.So, the sol-dier "bucket" can hold the gift of leadership. But, shepherd "bucket" might also contain the spiritual gift of leadership. The soldier "bucket" might hold the gift of teaching, but the servant "bucket" contains it too.

Certain spiritual gifts do cluster around certain pictures of Jesus, but there is not a direct correlation. The picture shows who God has made you to be. The spiritual gift is how he fills you as that person to carry out the mission he has given you.

ARE THE EIGHT PICTURES OF JESUS BIBLICAL?

Absolutely. After a thorough study of the Bible, we chose these eight pictures because they appeared in both the Old and New Testaments. The biblical writers repeat and explain them the most.

Since Jesus is the Word of God, any understanding of human personality apart from him in the Bible is certain to fail.

HOW HAVE YOU USED THE EIGHT PICTURES OF JESUS IN YOUR FAMILY LIFE?

The eight pictures of Jesus emerged from our exhaustive study of Jesus in the Bible. My wife and I wanted to know what our oldest son would be like if he was "like Jesus" when he walked across the stage at high school graduation. The pictures you have learned, however, began to shape and mold other parts of our family.

The eight pictures of Jesus helped us recognize the unique personality and passions of each of our four children and affirm them. Rather than a "one-size-fits-all" approach, we used the pictures as direction from Jesus on how to train each of our children up in the way God had made them.

We were also able to help our children deal with conflict better because they understood the different needs and drives of each picture. Each child became good at navigating different types of people and accepting them as created in the image of God. Exceptional leaders have this quality and use it to lead well. The eight pictures of Jesus also helped my wife and I keep our family on a consistent spiritual development plan. Before we discovered the eight pictures, we would try this and then try that, but nothing we planned ever lasted for long. After we began to apply the eight pictures within our family, each member of our family could tell you in a heartbeat how we were doing spiritually as a family. They could also tell you the direction we needed to go to become more like Jesus.

CONCLUSION

Most people have a hard time accepting themselves. They wish they were better at something, feel like they fall short of everyone else, or are over confident—until life deals a blow from which they think they may never recover. They hope their relationship with God will help them, but even then, come up short and feel far away from Jesus.

When you reach the end of yourself, only a close friendship with God in prayer can save you. In your darkest hours, powerful prayer will change your life in ways you could never imagine. Even now, you probably can think of times when drawing close to God was the only thing that helped you not lose your mind.

In this book, I have shown you a way to draw close to Jesus and receive the help you need. You discovered which of the eight different kinds of people you are. You learned why eight different types of people exist—people are created in the image of God and Jesus is the image of the invisible God. You learned scriptural insights about each picture (which I plan to share even more in my next book).

You can know your personality type and that Jesus is each picture perfectly and still fall short. Jesus said when his people remain in him, they will bear much fruit and experience unconditional, life-giving acceptance and love. That's what I need most in my life. I'm thinking you would say you need self-acceptance and love, too.

That's where the eight pictures of Jesus help. A picture is worth a thousand words. As you meditate on who Jesus is and pray as he prays, you change.

It takes time. God isn't in a rush. But it does happen. I've seen it in my life and the lives of others, too. I wrote this book because I want to see it in your life, as well. I look forward to hearing many stories in heaven of how God used these truths to transform you.

When I turned fifty years old, I looked back over years of being a husband, a father, a brother, a son, a friend, a pastor, and a missionary. Amid trials and difficulties, God blessed in incredible ways—much more than I ever deserved or could earn.

Several friends at the time asked me to share a sermon or blog post on how to live a life that God blesses. They wanted to know the bedrock truths that my wife and I had followed. What they were asking was "how can you live your life in such a way that you experience spiritual success"—not the fleeting success of fame, money, and possessions, but success that lasts forever.

Reflecting over almost forty years of walking with Jesus, four truths emerged: Listen, Obey, Value, and Empower, or L.O.V.E. — the key to a full life. Listening to God and the needs of others, obeying God by following the Great Commandment, valuing everyone's contribution, and empowering others to reach their full potential is what love looks like.

I share that story because the eight pictures of Jesus are like a compass that helps believers listen, obey, value, and empower.

Understanding people have different personalities that reflect Jesus (when they are in the Spirit!) will help you listen better. Obeying the Great Commandment which flows out of the heart of Jesus and knowing which of the pictures God made you will help you connect with God's heart. Accepting other's differences and learning how to work together will show others you value them. When you stop trying to be perfect and focus on helping those around you become better, people will feel loved and not judged.

Blessed living occurs when people feel heard, love God with their entire being, value everyone on the team, and depend on the power of the Holy Spirit to help each person reach their full potential.

Let Jesus take each of these pictures of himself and change you from the inside out. Take time when you finish reading and ask the Spirit of God to show you how he wants you to apply what you have learned. Let God sow this good seed into your heart and bring a harvest of thirty, sixty, or one-hundredfold.

> *Lord Jesus,*
>
> *Fill my friend to overflowing with your Spirit and presence.*
>
> *May they be like a soldier and win the spiritual battles they face by your grace and power.*

May they be like a seeker and find what they have been searching for all their life — real meaning, true joy, and perfect peace.

May they be like a shepherd and tend your lambs, feeding and protecting them from the wolves in this world.

May they be like a sower and plant your Word firmly in their own heart and the hearts of others—knowing your Word never returns without a harvest. May they be like a son or daughter and help those broken by divorce and untimely deaths to find a banquet table of love and family once again.

May they be like a saint and point others to your glory—reminding those who have given up hope that you are near and care.

May they be like a servant and walk in your anointing to preach the good news, heal the sick, and meet the practical needs no one else sees.

May they be like a steward and use all their resources— their time, their money, and their plans—to see your kingdom come and your will be done on earth.

All people struggle and make mistakes, Father, but bless my friend and wipe the tears from their eyes. Remove everything in their life holding them back.

May they know deep in their heart that someday they will be like Jesus and everything will be put right.

Even so, come quickly Jesus.

In your name. Amen

THANK YOU

Before you go, I'd like to say "thank you" again for purchasing my book and I hope you have been blessed by it. I know you could have picked from dozens of books, but you felt the Lord leading you to mine.

Again, a big thank you for downloading *Powerful Jesus in the War Room* and reading it to the end.

Could I ask a *small* favor? Please take a minute to leave a review for this book at go.lightkeeperbooks.com/e-pjw-rev

Think of your brief review as giving a short testimony that helps others know if this book is what they need to grow in their spiritual life.

Your review will help me continue to write Kindle books that help people grow in their walk with Jesus. And if you loved it, please let me know that too! :)

BONUS

Don't forget to download your free *Powerful Prayers Bonus Pak*! The free *Powerful Prayers Bonus Pak* includes three resources to help you pray powerful prayers:

- 100 Promises – Audio Version
- 40 Faith-Building Quotes
- 40 Powerful Prayers.

All are suitable for framing. Download your free *Powerful Prayers Bonus Pak* at go.lightkeeperbooks.com/powerpak

I've also included an excerpt from my book *Powerful Worship in the War Room*. God has blessed many through this book and I wanted to give you a chance to "try before you buy." To order *Powerful Worship in the War Room* visit go.lightkeeperbooks.com/e-pww

If you enjoyed *Powerful Jesus in the War Room*, please leave a review. Your feedback will help other believers find this book easier and encourage me in my calling to write practical, powerful books to encourage, equip, and empower Christians throughout the world.

POWERFUL WORSHIP
IN THE
WAR ROOM

DANIEL B LANCASTER PhD

INTRODUCTION

As many have learned and later taught, you don't realize Jesus is all you need until Jesus is all you have.

– TIM KELLER

Christianity sure seems complicated and cluttered today.

Everyone has an opinion about what you should or shouldn't do. There are books and tapes and sermons and church services and small groups, and the list goes on. Amid the swirl, I have often found myself in a spiritual desert and wondering how my life could be different.

Then I read what Paul said in 2 Corinthians 11:3: "I worry that you have left the simplicity of Christ." Maybe following Jesus should be simple after all.

That's what this book is all about. I want to show you how I and others have simplified our spiritual lives. A simple spiritual life is sustainable, nourishing, and will help you to flourish as a person.

My family spent 12 years on the mission field and learned many truths about ourselves and our walk with God. There's nothing like leaving your culture and being thrust into a completely new one to shake the chaff from the wheat! What we discovered disturbed us – many of the "truths" and "principles" we had heard in church all of our lives didn't work in another country. It led us to a crisis of belief.

That's when the simplicity of following Jesus became real to us. In this book, I want to share with you what we discovered. I believe it will set you free from the false expectations of cultural Christianity. You are going to be able to let go and let God take you places you could have never believed. Don't get me wrong, I still struggle in my walk with Jesus. But walking with Him in a simpler way has allowed me to find true north much easier and to move towards becoming a healthier person.

I'm going to share with you some of the same lessons we learned and taught to over 5,000 national believers in Southeast Asia. God worked in our friends to start over 1,200 discipleship groups and 200 churches. More than that, our family grew in Christ together amid incredibly difficult times.

I believe as you read and apply the simple spiritual habits we will talk about in this book, you are going to experience new freedom in your life. Not some emotional one-and-done, but continual rivers of living water. You will experience the joy of walking in simplicity with Jesus. As you de-clutter your life and live more simply, you will have more time for the relationships in life that really matter.

When God called our family of six to move overseas as missionaries, our children were eleven, nine, seven, and four years old at the time. That move was, as I'm sure you understand, a giant leap of faith.

We sold our house and two cars and gave most of our other belongings away. The country we moved to did not allow crates to be sent from the United States. It was considered one of the top five worst military dictatorships in the world.

As a result, our family packed everything into nineteen suitcases, boarded a plane, and left for Southeast Asia to start a new life. Although we left a few household memories in storage back in America, those nineteen suitcases represented a return to a simpler life.

Life was not easy. Soldiers with machine guns stood guard at every major intersection in the capital city. Insurgents detonated a bomb in a store my wife had left only thirty minutes earlier, killing seventeen of the clerks and managers. We removed three cobras from the front flower bed where our kids normally played. Secret police followed us everywhere and would question the national friends we spent time with after we had left their homes.

But many years later, our whole family will tell you it is the best move we ever made. Living overseas simplified our lives, drew us closer as a family, and strengthened our faith.

I can't think of a better time to simplify your life and find true happiness than right now, can you? The following pages will give you practical ways to simplify your spiritual life, make the changes into habits, and watch God transform your life.

If your spiritual life is cluttered and feels like a desert, I know that reading this will help you because it has helped me and others just like you. Let's start by looking at the foundation of a simple spiritual life – loving God.

1
LOVING GOD

Living simply makes loving simple.

— BELL HOOKS

Everyone wants to be loved and to love others. The problem is we have hurts, habits, and hang-ups that keep us from love. We end up feeling lonely, disconnected, and miserable.

In this chapter, I want to show you how to break the chains that are holding you back. We're going to look at the Great Commandment and see how God will heal you as you obey Him.

God loves you and wants you to experience His love. In fact, God is the source of love, so it is important you receive love from Him, so you can give love to the people in your life. Love problems are always God problems.

I come from a broken home and have found loving God, myself, and others difficult at times — that is until I started obeying the Great Commandment in practical ways. My wife and I taught our kids to do the same, and they continue to follow Jesus and share the love of God to this day. I also have seen what you will learn in this chapter transform thousands of people's lives.

When you finish reading this chapter, you will have learned a practical way to experience the love of God. You will have simple truths that you can fall back to when you are hurting, facing a crisis, or feeling betrayed by a friend. No matter where you find yourself in life, you will have a simple and powerful way to connect with God.

I remember a Bible training event that took place while we were missionaries in Southeast Asia. It was in a remote area that took three hours to reach by air, followed by a ten-hour bus trip to the foot of a mountain. Finally, we took a two-hour motorcycle ride to the village church that was hosting the training.

A few days before the start of the Bible training, I called the pastor and told him I would not be able to come. I had the flu with a high temperature, ached all over my body, and felt weak. We needed to postpone the training. His reply surprised me.

He said, "We can't postpone the training."

Usually, Asian pastors are gracious and don't address missionaries in a direct way like this. I knew for him to say "we can't" went against his culture and upbringing.\

I said, "You don't understand. I have the flu and a high temperature. My whole body is aching, and I feel weak."

He said, "I am sorry for that, brother. We will pray that God heals you, but we cannot postpone the training. Believers have been walking through the jungle for a week to attend the training, and I have no way to tell them we have canceled it. You must come."

I prayed about whether I should go or not again and ended up going to the training. We had twelve participants, and they started eleven churches in the following months. God gave me the strength to persevere.

During our time as foreign missionaries, we normally only saw local believers once. We traveled around the country and Southeast Asia, rarely returning to the same place a second time.

I realized this meant we likely only had one chance with each person. God pricked my heart, asking, "If you could train believers how to obey only one command of Jesus, which one would you choose?" One command? Teach and practice just ONE spiritual habit that would result in believers obeying all the rest of Jesus's commands?

Eventually, we decided the "one command" to teach was the Great Commandment. If a person simply obeyed the Great Commandment to love God with all their heart, soul, mind, and strength, they would flourish as a Christ-follower.

In this chapter, I will show you what we learned and taught our children and others. I'm excited because you are going to be blessed as you apply the Great Commandment in your life. God is going to bring healing, strength, confidence, and joy for you like He has many others.

So, let's look at the Great Commandment, and at how you can let God simplify your spiritual life.

THE GREAT COMMANDMENT

The first step in simplifying your spiritual life and strengthening your faith is experiencing the love of God.

Love is the cornerstone of real happiness and authentic spirituality. The more you receive and give love, the deeper you will grow spiritually. My prayer is that you will find greater love in your life.

Unfortunately, true love is hard to come by for most people. And that leads us to do desperate things while trying to find love, even when we know those choices will hurt us. Satan uses this against us all the time. He tempts us to sin and laughs in glee when we do, knowing we feel even more unlovable and unloved by God. I don't have to tell you it can be a vicious cycle and hard to overcome.

Deep down we know that love is the answer to our problem, but we often feel helpless or unable to love or be loved. We try hard but fail. I used to think I had to love through my own effort. Thankfully, God has provided another way. The Bible says in I John 4:7-8:

> *Dear friends, let us love one another, because love is from God, and everyone who loves has been born of God and knows God. The one who does not love does not know God, because God is love. (HCSB)*

The good news is that love comes from God first. When we love God or another person, we are merely taking the love we have already received from God and giving it away.

We receive love from God and give love back to Him. We receive love from God and give it to others. Simple. Powerful. This is how God created love to work.

When we find it hard to love God or people, typically we aren't receiving or accepting enough of the love of God in our life. The problem isn't that we can't give love, but that we haven't received enough love to be able to give love away. We will return to this spiritual principle many times in this book.

It is important to keep the "we receive love to give love" principle in mind when you read the Great Commandment in Mark 12:38-41:

> *One of the teachers of the law came and heard them debating. Noticing that Jesus had given them a good answer, he asked Him, "Of all the commandments, which is the most important?" "The most important one," answered Jesus, "is this: 'Hear, O Israel, the Lord our God, the Lord is one. Love the Lord your God with all your heart and with all your soul and with all your mind and with all your strength.' The second is this: 'Love your neighbor as yourself.' There is no commandment greater than these."*

Jesus shares the most important command that anyone can obey: love God with everything you are and do. Considering the Pharisees of the time taught that "true believers" had to obey 633 different commands, Jesus simplified everything quite a bit.

Let's look at how we can obey the command to love God with all our heart, soul, mind, and strength. Obeying the Great Commandment is the key to finding true love.

WITH YOUR HEART

Loving God with all your heart means that you love Him with that part of you that feels deeply, that hopes and cares, and that is burdened when your life isn't right.

The hand motion for loving God with all your heart is pictured below. Put both of your hands on your heart.

The first part of the Great Commandment is loving God with all your heart.

Your heart can be broken, hurting, and closed – or – your heart can be open, full, and overflowing. God sent His Son, so your heart could be free and flowing like a river of living water. That is God's will for you.

I can remember times in my life when my heart was light, and I felt like I was walking on clouds. I felt a great love for everyone and felt great joy. Those times make the best memories a person can have while living in this broken world. You can probably remember times like those in your life, too.

Sadly, though, troubles weighed my heart down much of the time and made it hard to love God. I hope you haven't experienced that, but I know that most people have.

Satan shackles our heart in so many ways. Maybe when you were growing up, it wasn't OK to share how you really felt, and this locked your heart down. Or maybe you found yourself in situations where you had to "perform" for others and didn't feel like you could be the real you, so your heart developed walls to protect yourself. I've listed just a few examples of the shackles that can make it hard to love God with all our heart.

One of the ways people deal with their heart pain is by trying to fill their lives with accomplishments or material possessions to prove they are valuable. Surely, they think "if I do valuable work or have wealth, I am valuable myself." What ends up happening, however, is hurting people who are over-committed at work and overwhelmed with credit card debt. Their lives have become complicated and confusing, and they feel trapped.

So, you hear this command and think "I would like to love God with all my heart, but I don't think I can. I have too much hurt holding me back." There is a way to simplify your life, and it starts with loving God with all your heart. And it is easier than you might think.

God is love, and His heart's desire is that you experience His love. True love always brings healing. The more time you spend with God and let Him love you, the more you will be healed and be able to return His love.

Picture yourself walking in a forest filled with tall trees and beautiful flowers. The forest is quiet except for the sweet sound of birds calling. As you walk along the path, you see a mountain spring and decide to sit down and enjoy the relaxing sound of the water running across the rocks.

You feel your heart become strangely warm as Jesus sits down beside you. Both of you are quiet for several minutes, just enjoying each other's company and watching the mountain spring.

Then Jesus turns and says, "Tell me what is on your heart."

At first, you share just a little because your experience with other people has been that they don't really want to hear everything. So, you aren't sure if Jesus wants to hear about the feelings you want to share. You think that maybe He is just saying that.

During your conversation, however, He says "tell me more" several times, and you finally understand that He truly wants to know you, the real you. He loves you and wants to hear about everything on your heart.

You feel the fears begin to melt away; the perfectionism begins to loosen its hold; and the desire for anything but sharing time with Jesus fades. You see clearly how empty performing to prove yourself is. You see how the things you own have really been owning you.

Rivers of living water flow from your heart. Rivers of love flow between you and Jesus.

As you get up to walk home, Jesus smiles and gives you a hug.

"Let My heart heal your heart," He says.

You go home with a heart that wants to love God and love others. Loving is simpler than you thought.

Anytime you feel your heart is hard and pulling away from God, it is a sign that you have allowed your heart to become cluttered. Let perfectionism and wanting more possessions fall to the side and accept a God-healed heart.

Jesus doesn't expect you to come to Him perfectly; He just wants to spend time with you because He loves you. He knows you have tried to fill the hole in your heart with glitter and gold. But He doesn't condemn. Jesus wants you to simplify your life, so you will have more time with Him and the people you love.

Let me encourage you to go today to the stream that never runs dry and find that wonderful living water for your parched heart. God will help you and heal you as you love Him with all your heart.

WITH YOUR SOUL

The next part of the Great Commandment is to love God with all your soul. Bible scholars debate what the soul is and its location in the human body. In fact, scholars have many differing opinions. With so much disagreement, how can we decide how to love God with all our soul?

For me, I look at how Jesus lived and what He said about the soul. Jesus prayed in the Garden of Gethsemane the night before He was crucified, saying "My soul is greatly distressed unto death" (Matthew 26:38). I don't know about you, but when I am praying fervently, I feel something in my stomach. For that reason, this is the hand motion we use to depict loving God with all your soul:

Now, I'm not saying some people have bigger souls than other folks. Nor am I saying if you are thin you have a small soul. What I am saying is one of the places the soul expresses itself is in your stomach. It is the place you feel when you are praying like you have never prayed before. Some examples of these times are after you learn of a dear friend's auto accident or perhaps find out a family member has a major illness.

Some people sell their soul to the devil, while other people are called "kind souls". You can have an old soul, a tired soul, or be a kindred soul. You can bare your soul or pour out your soul, and confession is good for the soul. Maybe you are the life and soul of the party or people call you a soul brother.

I think our soul is that part of us that gives us willpower and the ability to keep going in difficult times. The soul helps us keep commitments our minds have decided are important. That is why Jesus also prayed in the Garden of Gethsemane, "Not my will, but Thine" (Matthew 26:39). Your soul has a deep sense of the mission God sent you into this world to fulfill.

When our family learned that my wife had ovarian cancer, I felt like all the wind had been taken out of my sails. I lost all motivation and energy. My soul grieved, and everything turned gray and gloomy. Have you experienced something life-shattering like that before? If you have, I pray that God will somehow help you see the sunshine again.

Sadly, it is easy for our broken world to damage your soul. You may have given up on your life. You may have said,

"Nothing I do matters any way. Everything always turns out wrong." You may have found yourself thinking the world would be a better place if you weren't alive. Like George Bailcy in the movie It's a Wonderful Life, you may find yourself saying, "I want to live again. I want to live again."

We as humans try several coping strategies when our soul is damaged. Some people decide they must take life by the reins - become the master of their soul – and try to control everything. Others want to escape life and the suffering in their soul, so they disconnect with drugs, or alcohol, or pornography, or anything that helps them forget the pain.

The problem is... none of this works. Controlling things and people may work for a while, but soon the soul begins to cry out for something more. Trying to escape life ends in bondage. Many people find themselves empty after trying these coping strategies and still searching. If we are honest, we are all in that place more than we like to admit.

You can purchase *Powerful Worship in the War Room* at go.lightkeeperbooks.com/e-pww.

MORE FROM THIS AUTHOR

#1 Best Sellers
on
amazon

This series on powerful prayer, heart-felt worship, and intimacy with Christ will help strengthen your "War Room" and give you a battle plan for prayer.

Visit go.lightkeeperbooks.com/battleplan to learn more.

CHRISTIAN SELF-HELP

Available on amazon

Overcome fear, shame, and other spiritual attacks that hold you back from being all God created you to be.

Visit go.lightkeeperbooks.com/selfhelp to learn more

Coming Soon

SATAN IS A LIAR
Satan only cares about himself and stopping you. Learn how to overcome the greatest narcissist of all time.

Lightkeeper Kids Series

Available On
amazon

"Very sweet! Easy for kids to understand and relate to!"

Visit **go.lightkeeperbooks.com/lkk** to learn more

ABOUT THE AUTHOR

Daniel B Lancaster (PhD) enjoys training others to become passionate followers of Christ. He has planted two churches in America and trained over 5,000 people in Southeast Asia as a strategy coordinator with the International Mission Board. He served as Assistant Vice-President for University Ministries at Union University and currently is a international missionary with Cornerstone International. He has four grown children and a delightful grandson.

Dr. Dan is available for speaking and training events. Contact him at dan@lightkeeperbooks.com to arrange a meeting for your group.

Printed in Great Britain
by Amazon